Big Wishes
and Her Baby

By Margie Sigman
Illustrated by Jason Cheshire

Scott Foresman
is an imprint of

PEARSON

Glenview, Illinois • Boston, Massachusetts • Chandler, Arizona •
Upper Saddle River, New Jersey

Photographs

Every effort has been made to secure permission and provide appropriate credit for photographic material. The publisher deeply regrets any omission and pledges to correct errors called to its attention in subsequent editions.

Unless otherwise acknowledged, all photographs are the property of Pearson Education, Inc.

12 Momatiuk – Eastcott/Corbis.

ISBN 13: 978-0-328-50754-2
ISBN 10:   0-328-50754-7

10   V010   15 14 13

My name is Lori. My mom has a riding school. The school is near our house. I think it's the best school of all.

My mom teaches kids about riding. Big Wishes is my mom's horse. She is a very good horse.

SCHOO

Big Wishes is a mom too! She had a baby horse in the spring. It's a girl, like me.

Today, my friends drove here in their car. This is the first day the baby horse can have visitors. She is old enough now.

Big Wishes is a very good mom. She watches my friends with her baby. The baby loves to play tag. She runs away from us!

Every day we take care of the horses. We put out hay for them. We put grain in their buckets.

We also brush each horse.
Mom has lots of brushes. Horses
love to be brushed.

Mom mixes special food for the baby horse. She mashes oats with milk. The food helps the baby grow.

Mom said I can name our new horse. Some horses have names like Patches. Others have names like Star or Midnight. What do you think would be a good name?

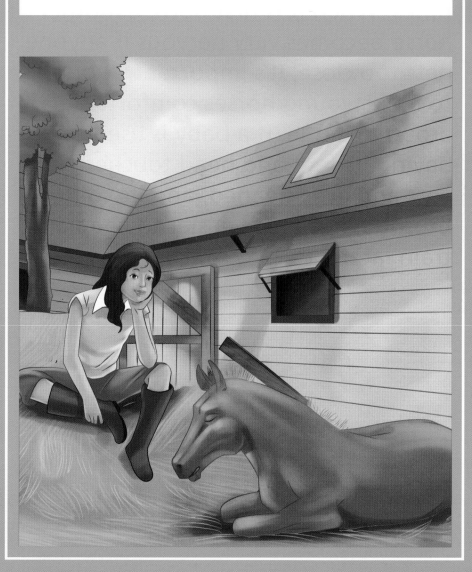

Some Facts About Horses

Most mares, or female horses, are very good mothers. They keep a careful eye on their babies at all times. When it is first born, a mother horse becomes very nervous if anyone gets too close. It's important, though, to make young horses comfortable around people. If a baby is used to having its feet and head touched, its ears and eyes cleaned, and its coat brushed, it is much easier to keep and train later on.